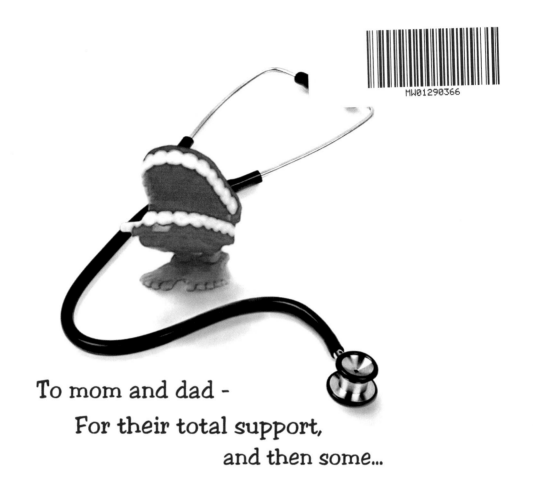

To mom and dad -
For their total support,
and then some...

I once dreamed that I was a bug

Deep down

in a carpet I dug

And now I know why

I hear folks reply,

"I'm as snug as a bug in a rug!"

There once was a young crocodile

Who valued her beautiful smile

She brushed her whole mouth
From the north to the south

But it certainly took her a while!

I started to hiccup today

The darn things just won't go away

My brother yelled, "Boo!"

since that's what you do

At least that's what *some* people say!

Two turtles named Rufus and Zeke

Decided to play hide and seek

Zeke looked high and low

But since he moved slow

Finding Rufus took nearly a week!

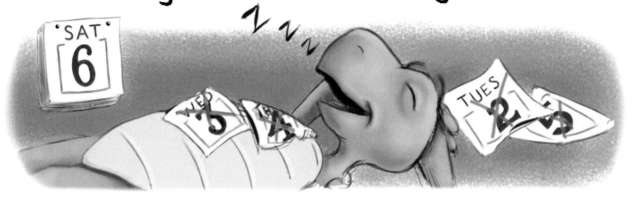

Slurpy McGrew loved his noodles

And so did his
little french poodles

They ate them all day

"How much?" did you say?

I heard from a friend, "It's just oodles!"

My dog ate my homework last night

My math problems - every last bite

I would have been mad

But it's not so bad

I don't think I got many right!

A snowman I made on my lawn

Looked different this morning at dawn

I once had a chat with a pig

Who was wearing a curly brown wig

But when I asked why

She just gave a sigh

And said the blonde one was too big!

His feet left the ground
He flew all around

'Til gram said, "Come down on the double!"

Just now an idea's occured -

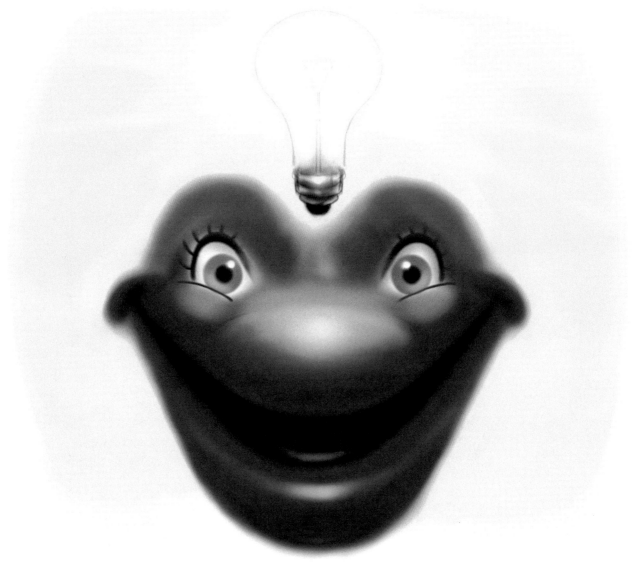

If you like the limericks you've heard

Just read them again

with a grownup
and then

Next time, *you* guess the last word!

The End